Learn About

YOUR BEST SELF

I Can Be Honest

written by Meredith Rusu

illustrated by Alexandra Colombo

Children's Press®
An imprint of Scholastic Inc.

Special thanks to Doctor Ann (Nancy) Close, Assistant Professor of the Yale School of Medicine and member of the Child Study Center at Yale University, for her insight into the development of children in early childhood.

Library of Congress Cataloging-in-Publication Data available
ISBN 978-93-5954-644-5

This reprint edition: September, 2025

Printed in India at Shiv Shakti Printing & Trading Co., Haryana

Book design by Kathleen Petelinsek

TABLE OF CONTENTS

I Can Be Honest

Hi! My name is Kylie. Do you know what it means to be honest?

I do! When I'm honest, it makes me feel happy and proud. **HONESTY MATTERS** a whole lot! But it is not always easy... Let me show you!

TIGER

I can be honest by telling the truth about if I brushed my teeth.

I didn't feel like brushing them.

But I know it's wrong to pretend I did and **fib**.

When I do brush my teeth, it feels good telling Mommy!

HONESTY MATTERS

Mommy says she can trust me!

I can be honest by bringing back the classroom stuffed animal I borrowed.

Our class rules say that we can only take one home if we promise to bring it back.

And I kept my **promise**!

HONESTY MATTERS

My teacher says "thank you"!

UFFED ANIMAL
LIBRARY
Tiger
Turtle
Panda

milk
milk
milk

I can be honest by not cutting in line at lunch.

The lunch aide thinks I was first.

And my tummy is rumbling, so I kind of do want to go first.

But it's only fair to wait my turn.

HONESTY MATTERS

The lunch aide says I'm a very **considerate** student.

I can be honest by admitting I cheated during a board game.

I wanted to win, and I thought I could be sneaky.

But cheating made me feel **ashamed**.

No one wants to play with a cheater.

HONESTY MATTERS

My friends give me another chance. I feel happier playing fair and square.

LIBRAR
ROCK D
SPECIAL DOG
BUGS
BUGS
ROCK THE DOG
SPECIAL DOG

I can be honest about which book I want to pick at the library.

Even though my friends all like one series, I like something completely different.

And that's okay!

HONESTY MATTERS

The librarian helps me find LOTS of books that I like! That makes me feel special.

I can be honest by not grabbing a toy from the Friday Prize Jar without permission.

My friends dared me to.

But stealing isn't right.

HONESTY MATTERS

I feel extra happy when the teacher says I earned a prize.

HEAD
THORAX
ABDOMEN

BUGS
BUGS
KYLIE ON BOARD
BEST DAD
23

I can be honest when Daddy asks me how school was, and I tell him everything.

The good and even the not-so-good stuff.

HONESTY MATTERS

Daddy says he's very proud of how hard I'm working at school.

I can be honest by not tricking my little brother, Billy, into thinking there's a monster in his closet.

I like being silly.

But Billy believes what I say, and it's not nice to tease him.

HONESTY MATTERS

Billy gives me a hug and says, "I love you!"

GER

I can be honest by telling my parents about a bad dream I had.

It's difficult to explain something that feels scary.

But if I don't try to tell them, they won't know.

HONESTY MATTERS

My parents set up a night-light for me so I'm not as scared.

Did you see? Being honest is not always easy. But when I'm honest, other people can trust me.

And I can trust myself.

That makes me feel safe, happy, and loved!

HONESTY MATTERS!

Honesty is very important in every **friendship**. In order to be friends, you need to know someone will be fair, truthful, and trustworthy.

Read the examples below together with a grown-up. Which ones show honesty? Which ones don't? How would you feel about each kid?

1

Every time Julia comes over, she takes one of your toys home without asking.

2

Juan promises you can go on the monkey bars first at recess. When you get to the playground, he does let you go first.

3

Suzanne realizes she miscounted the cards during a game. She asks if you can start over because she made a mistake.

4

Hector draws a picture on the wall with a marker. Then he tells the teacher that you drew it!

5

Ms. Blanco accidentally gives Ruby more crackers than you at snack time. Ruby sees you got less and offers to share her extras.

ANSWERS: Numbers 2, 3, and 5 show honesty. Numbers 1 and 4 don't show honesty.

HONESTY IS KIND

Is it possible to be too honest? Yes! Sometimes, saying exactly what you think or feel can hurt other people's feelings. That's when you may have been too honest.

Read the examples below together with an adult. Which ones do you think are too honest? What could each kid have said instead to be honest and kind at the same time?

1

Giada sings a song she's been practicing. Alexa doesn't think it sounds very good. She tells Giada her singing hurts her ears.

2

Tommy's aunt offers him ketchup on his hamburger. Tommy says he doesn't really like ketchup and asks if he could please have mustard instead.

3

Naomi hears people speaking in a different language. She thinks it sounds funny and asks them why they're talking weird.

4

Rocco is at a birthday party, but his tummy is starting to hurt. When a parent offers him birthday cake, he says, "No, thank you— I don't feel like any."

5

Mitch's little brother does a shape-sorter puzzle. Mitch thinks that's too easy and says he's playing with "baby toys."

ANSWER: Numbers 1, 3, and 5 are hurtful and *too* honest.

GLOSSARY

ashamed (uh-SHAYMD) feeling embarrassed and guilty

Julie felt ashamed when she was caught sneaking a cookie before dinner.

considerate (kuhn-SID-ur-it) careful and concerned for other people's needs and feelings

It was considerate of Jimmy to hold the door open for his teacher.

earned (URND) to get something that you deserve

She earned a gold star by being a good student.

fib to tell a small lie

Even though I hadn't eaten my carrots, I told a fib and said I had.

friendship (FREND-ship) the relationship between you and someone you like and know well

Our friendship is strong—we always play together!

promise (PRAH-mis) to declare that you will definitely do a particular thing, or that a particular thing will happen

I promise to clean up my mess.

trust (TRUHST) to believe that someone is honest and reliable

I trust people who do what they say they will.

ABOUT THE AUTHOR

Meredith Rusu has written more than 100 children's books. She lives in New Jersey with her husband and two young sons whom she tries (very hard!) to inspire to be honest every day.

ABOUT THE ILLUSTRATOR

Alexandra Colombo has illustrated more than 100 books that have been published all over the world. She loves walking in the woods, writing poetry, and discovering new places. She lives in Italy with her dog, Ary, and her turtle, Carlo.